# PRODUCTION AND ITS EFFECTS

# THE SOUTHERN PERSPECTIVES ON DEVELOPMENT SERIES

**Book 1: Starting Points**

The power of words and images -- What is development? -- The creation of poverty -- Interdependence.

**Book 2: Colonialism and its Legacy**

The South before colonialism -- European expansion -- Social and economic impacts -- Independence and neocolonialism.

**Book 3: Distribution of People and Resources**

Levels of consumption -- Food -- Health -- Population.

**Book 4: Production and its Effects**

Work -- The transnational economy -- Migration and urbanisation -- Technology and sustainability.

**Book 5: Rights and Choices**

Human rights -- Models of development -- Questioning aid -- Working for change.

The materials are designed to be used flexibly according to your needs. However, it is strongly recommended that students have a grounding in the main ideas of Books 1 and 2 before attempting to cover the issues in Books 3, 4 and 5.

# CONTENTS

Key ideas at a glance ............................................. page 4

Foreword .............................................................. page 6

Introduction ......................................................... page 7

Section A: Work .................................................... page 9

Section B: The transnational economy ................. page 21

Section C: Migration and urbanisation ................. page 39

Section D: Technology and sustainability ............. page 57

Recommended resources ..................................... page 71

About DEP ........................................................... page 72

# BOOK 4

## KEY IDEAS AT A GLANCE

### SECTION A: WORK

4.1 Work can be defined in different ways. Work does not always have a monetary reward.

4.2 Women (with the help of children) produce over half the world's wealth, yet much of their work is unpaid and unrecognised.

### SECTION B: THE TRANSNATIONAL ECONOMY

4.3 The international mobility of capital is a key feature of the global economy. Multinational companies (MNCs) play a central role in this process.

4.4 MNCs, through the large size of their operations, have considerable influence on production and consumption in both the North and the South.

4.5 Industrial production has spread to many parts of the South, but has not benefited the majority of people there (eg. MNCs' use of Export Processing Zones).

4.6 In agricultural production, a small number of MNCs engaged in "agribusiness" increasingly control land and food worldwide.

## SECTION C: MIGRATION AND URBANISATION

4.7 Increasing poverty, landlessness and lack of livelihood in rural areas can push people to leave and try to find employment in urban areas (or in other countries).

4.8 Cities are often unable to accommodate all those seeking jobs. Many people end up trying to make a living in the "informal economy".

4.9 The pressures of migration and urban life have tended to undermine traditional family patterns and ways of life in the South.

## SECTION D: TECHNOLOGY AND SUSTAINABILITY

4.10 Technology which is researched and developed in one place is not necessarily right for other places. When introduced into the South, much Northern technology has proved unsuitable to the needs of its users and harmful to the environment.

4.11 Western concepts of land use and farming methods (eg. Green Revolution, large-scale farming, privatisation of common land) are seldom appropriate for the needs of the majority of farmers in the South.

4.12 Local problem-solving and technology which fits local needs and circumstances are key steps towards sustainable development.

# FOREWORD

The five-book series which includes this publication is the fruit of a two-year project, run by DEP from January 1994 to January 1996. The project arose from a realisation that there were a great many resources produced **about** the South; very few produced **with** the South. "Southern Perspectives" has involved a close collaboration between DEP and partners from the South, both individuals and organisations, to gather firsthand views and analyses of development issues. The resulting materials aim to provide for secondary students a rounded picture of what development means.

The principle behind the project, as in DEP's other work (see page 72), is that we must actively seek out and listen to Southern voices, and encourage in ourselves and our students an openness to engaging in North-South dialogue. In this way we can begin to challenge false perceptions and create more positive and better informed attitudes, leading to action for a more just world.

## A note on terminology

The first hurdle one must cross in producing materials such as this is how to refer to different parts of the world. There are various debates about terms such as "First World/Third World", "developed/ developing/less developed/underdeveloped countries" and so on. In this series, we have chosen to use the terms North and South. Although not geographically precise, they are less value-laden than many of the alternatives and are the current favourites amongst many activists and educators around the world.

We recognise that North and South are not the terms used in the National Curriculum for England and Wales, but our priority has been to listen to people from the places concerned. Students should be encouraged to become familiar with these terms and to think about why they matter. The debate about terms is taken up as a topic in its own right in Section A of Book 1.

# INTRODUCTION

The "Southern Perspectives on Development" series is designed mainly to support the teaching of Geography at Key Stages 3 and 4. It also includes useful material for History, English and Humanities.

Many of the issues covered are relevant to Religious Education and Personal and Social Education, and to cross-curricular themes such as Environmental Education and Citizenship. Using material from the series will enable teachers to contribute to the school's provision of "a broadly based curriculum which promotes the spiritual, moral, cultural, mental and physical development of pupils at the school and of society" (Education Reform Act 1988).

Teachers can use the Key Ideas for each book to guide the planning process and help them select the material most suitable for their subject or theme. The photocopiable students' pages provide numerous ready-to-use exercises to check understanding. These are supported by teachers' pages containing background information and ideas for activities, along with suggestions for differentiation and extension.

**Book 4** provides material to support the teaching of Key Stage 3 Geography Thematic Studies and GCSE Geography and Humanities. Material can also be used to look at issues of appropriate technology within the Key Stage 3 and 4 Design and Technology curriculum.

Geography

• The book provides essential material for teaching the Key Stage 3 Thematic Study of Development, particularly about differences in development and their effect on the quality of life of different groups of people, and how the interdependence of countries influences development. An investigative approach is encouraged.

• The book provides helpful material for teaching the Key Stage 3 Thematic Studies of Population, Settlement, and Economic Activities, particularly the causes and effects of migration, urban land use and the changes in distribution of economic activities.

• There is evidence-based material to investigate Environmental Issues, particularly considerations of sustainable development.

• Geographical skills of selecting and using secondary sources of evidence are particularly supported.

Cross-curricular Themes

• The book would provide useful material for <u>Environmental Education</u> and <u>Economic and Industrial Understanding.</u>

Book 4 covers agricultural and industrial production, and its implications both locally and globally. Economic activities are considered in a range of contexts, from women's unpaid work within the home to the activities of vast multinational corporations which look upon the whole world as their market. The informal economy becomes the focus in an investigation of urbanisation. Finally, questions are raised about what constitutes appropriate and sustainable technology in farming and industry.

The first section enables students to define the characteristics of work and to consider the distribution of different types of work. The unpaid contributions of women and the issue of child labour are particular subjects of investigation.

Section B moves to the global scale to examine the size and power of multinational corporations and their impact in areas such as the environment, health and safety and workers' rights. The agribusiness sector is used as an example of MNCs' influence on both producers and consumers.

The economic theme continues in Section C, with a consideration of the pressures towards migration and urbanisation. Statistics about urban growth worldwide are used alongside individual case studies illustrating some of the realities of modern urban life.

The final section includes an evaluation of the Green Revolution, with students being asked to weigh up its successes and failures. This forms part of a wider exploration of the meaning of technology and sustainability.

# SECTION A: WORK

## KEY IDEAS

4.1 Work can be defined in different ways. Work does not always have a monetary reward.

4.2 Women (with the help of children) produce over half the world's wealth, yet much of their work is unpaid and unrecognised.

## BACKGROUND

What do we mean by "work"? What are the rewards? Who does what?

We need to convey that work is much more than a 9-to-5 job for which one receives wages. It covers labour undertaken in a whole range of contexts: inside the home, out in the fields and so on.

Students should recognise the value of different kinds of work, including the unpaid work of women. This builds on related themes in earlier books, including how women's work is often left out of GNP calculations (Book 1); the disproportionate burden placed on women by Structural Adjustment Programmes (Book 2); and the contributions of women as producers of food and providers of health care (Book 3).

## SUGGESTED ACTIVITIES

The symbol ✪ on students' pages indicates more challenging tasks or questions, suitable for more able students.

The first necessary task in this section is to establish what "work" is. This could be done by means of a brainstorm, or the examples given on page 12 could be used as a starting point, with students adding their own ideas. Alternatively students could be asked to cut out pictures from newspapers and magazines and make a collage/display of types of work.

**Page 13** The motivations listed can be copied and cut up for diamond ranking in pairs or small groups.

Extension: Students write up their conclusions, giving reasons for the choices they have made.

**Page 15** Before revealing the information, you could list the 5 countries and ask students to guess which has the highest percentage of the work force in each of the three sectors. They could also try to predict which 2 have the same percentage engaged in industry -- is the answer surprising? More able students might look at the statistics with the list of countries removed and mixed up, and guess which country matches which set of figures.

**Page 16** Students can start with their own families for this topic: how do their mothers, aunts, grandmothers spend their time? What tasks do they do? A timeline of a female relative's day could be prepared. This could be broadened into a class "division of labour" report: students investigate which tasks are done by whom in their household (list tasks like cooking, shopping, cleaning, car maintenance etc., divided into which are done by whom) and then a cumulative class profile could be compiled. Given the range of possible family types it might be advisable to divide the categories of people into female adult/male adult/female children/male children rather than mother/father etc. [Source of statistics: *New Internationalist,* March 1988.]

**Page 17** Students could design a poster for the Wages for Housework campaign.

**Page 18** See also page 53 about children in Peru, and the exercise on "Useful children" in Section D, Book 3. It may be helpful to bring in a UK historical perspective by making a comparison with child labour during the Industrial Revolution.

**Page 20** This role play is based on the *Guardian Education* article, "All work, no play", 7.2.95. Students taking on the six roles can act as witnesses testifying on the issue of whether child labour should be banned. This could be done in groups, with a seventh person in each group taking on the role of cross-examiner challenging the testimony, or as a whole class with one set of performers making up a "Question Time" type of panel. Conclusions and reasons could be written up afterwards.

An alternative to acting out the role play would be for students to imagine that they have interviewed the people on the cards and then to write a newspaper report or feature article.

# Work

**?** Which of the following do you consider to be "work"? Why or why not?

* writing an essay for school

* writing a letter to your boyfriend/girlfriend

* playing football or tennis with friends

* playing football or tennis for money

* cleaning your own house

* cleaning someone else's house

* buying vegetables at the supermarket

* growing your own vegetables.

Add some examples of your own to show what you think counts as work.

✪ Which of these activities would count in Gross National Product? Remember that GNP includes only goods and services exchanged for money.

Why do people work?  What do they get out of it?

 With a partner, rank the following possible reasons:

| To ensure survival (food, shelter) for self/family | To change their environment or circumstances |
| --- | --- |
| To learn and develop themselves | To make a contribution to society |
| To gain independence | To be able to buy nice things |
| To reach a high position | To meet people |
| For self-respect | (Add an idea of your own if you wish.) |

A) Work ....13

# What kinds of work are there?

* Nearly half the work in the world is done in **agriculture**, to produce and prepare food.

* Most people in so-called "industrial" countries don't actually work in industry, but in offices and **services**: banking, shopkeeping, clerical work, health, education, transport and so on.

### % of labour force (1986-89) engaged in

|  | agriculture | industry | services |
|---|---|---|---|
| World | 48.5 | 16.3 | 35.2 |
| "Industrial" | 11.0 | 26.9 | 62.1 |
| "Developing" | 60.9 | 12.7 | 26.2 |

Source: *Human Development Report*, UNDP, 1992.

✏ Using information from the table above, shade in the pie charts to show how the labour force is divided in the given areas.

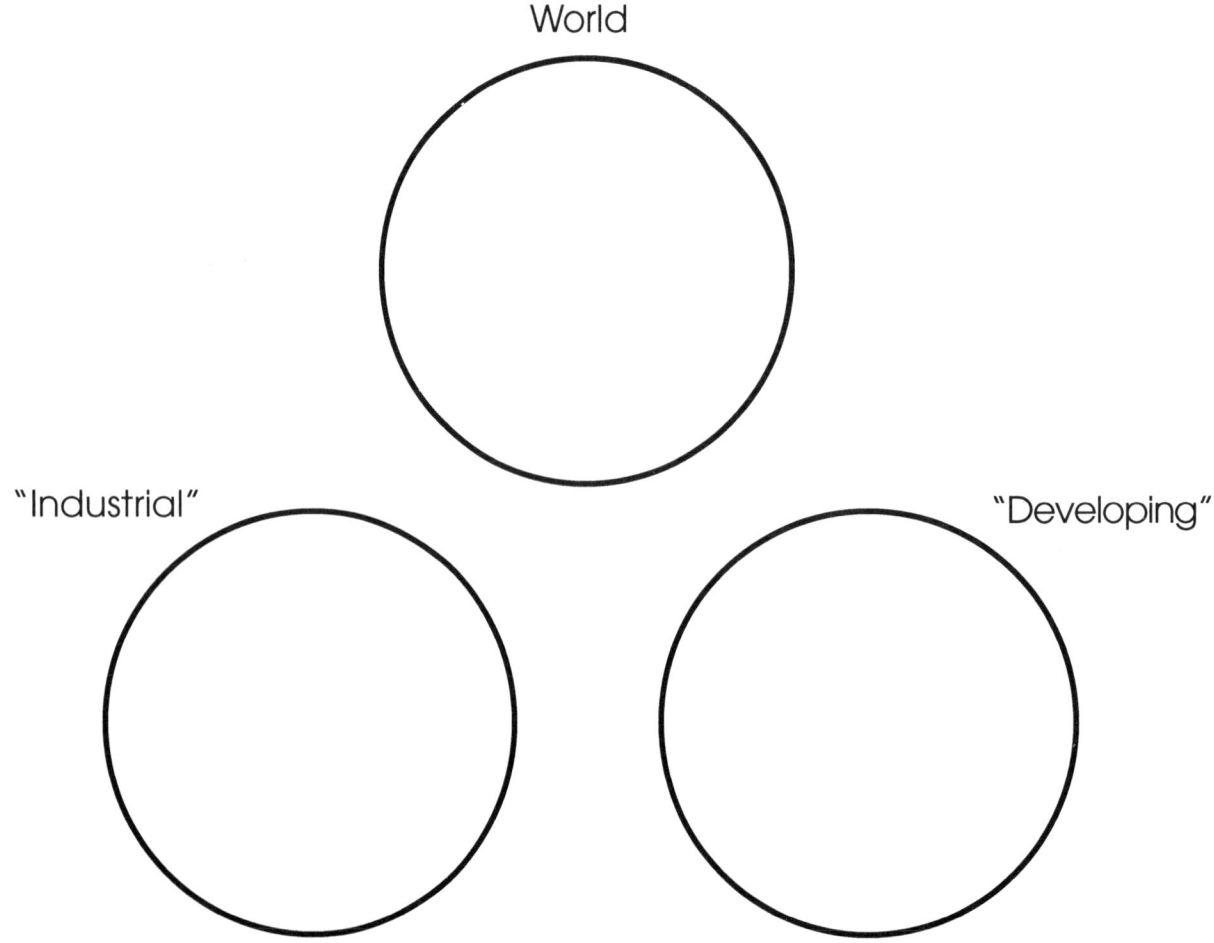

14.... BOOK 4 -- PRODUCTION AND ITS EFFECTS

| % of work force (in selected countries 1985-88) engaged in | | | |
| --- | --- | --- | --- |
| | agriculture | industry | services |
| India | 62.6 | 10.8 | 26.6 |
| Mexico | 22.9 | 20.1 | 57.0 |
| Poland | 28.5 | 38.9 | 32.6 |
| Tanzania | 85.6 | 4.5 | 9.9 |
| UK | 2.1 | 20.1 | 77.8 |

Source: *Third World Guide 1993-4.*

 Use the information above and on page 14 to answer the following questions.

1a  Of the 5 countries above, which one has the highest percentage of the labour force working in agriculture?

1b  In industry?

1c  In services?

2a  Which two countries have the same percentage working in industry?

2b  How do the agriculture and services figures for those two countries compare?

3  Which country above most closely matches the labour force profile of a "developing" country? (See page 14.)

4  Give three examples of jobs in the services sector. (See page 14.)

# Women and work

Women (with the help of children) produce over half the world's wealth, yet much of their work is unpaid and unrecognised.

* Carrying water in Tanzania takes 4 hours of a woman's time each day.
* Grinding grain, by hand, for a family in Mexico takes up to 6 hours a day.
* In India grinding grain takes 1.3 hours a day even when a mill is available.
* In Indonesia women spend over 3 hours a day just preparing food.

Fill in the table using the information above.

| Country | Task | Hours per day |
|---|---|---|
|  |  |  |
|  |  |  |
|  |  |  |
|  |  |  |

Assume seven hours' sleep per night. What percentage of her waking hours might a woman spend on each of the tasks listed above?

 Results of five major studies in villages in Tanzania, Burkina Faso, Bangladesh, Indonesia (Java) and Nepal showed that in all of these countries, men worked between 40 and 75 hours a week, but women's workload was always heavier by up to 21 more hours a week.

* Women with small children in the UK devote 50 hours a week to child-care alone.
* Women's unwaged work, estimated to produce as much as 50% of GNP worldwide, has been left out.
* Groups like the International Wages for Housework Campaign think that this is unfair. They say,

**❝ Women count -- count women's work. ❞**

Women's work is often not valued outside the home, either. Women tend to have jobs like the kind of work they do inside the home.

✎ Draw lines to connect the following household tasks with the paid jobs which they are like.

| | |
|---|---|
| preparing food | nurse |
| serving food | childminder |
| cleaning and tidying | cook |
| keeping accounts, paying bills | clerk |
| looking after children | maid/cleaner |
| caring for elderly parents | waitress |

How well paid are the jobs on the right? How well respected are they?

---

### Women's pay compared to men's

According to the Department of Employment's Earnings Survey, September 1994, the average pay for women working full-time was only 72% of the average for men of £362.10 a week.

---

✎ Use the information above to work out the average weekly pay for women working full-time.

✵ Can you suggest any possible reasons for the pay gap?

At the final World Conference of the UN Decade for Women in Nairobi in 1985, governments agreed that "The paid and, in particular, the unpaid contributions of women to all aspects and sectors of development should be recognised".

# Children's work

Children also work hard. One of the important contributions made by children in the South, particularly girls, is in doing time-consuming chores like collecting firewood and water, and looking after their younger brothers and sisters. This enables adults to go out and work at growing food or earning money.

**?** What other tasks can you think of that children might do?

What paid or unpaid work have you and your friends done?

✏ Use the article on page 19 to answer the following questions.

* According to the 1991 survey, what proportion of Birmingham school children were working?

* How many UK children work part-time?

* How does the UK compare with other European countries on the numbers of children working?

* What is allowed under the European Directive on child labour?

* How did the British government react to the new European law?

* At what age might children in India start working to make carpets?

* Under what conditions do the children work?

* Who buys the carpets?

✺ "Child labour is a Southern problem, and it is up to people in the South to sort it out." Do you agree or disagree? Give reasons for your answer.

# All work, no play

Guardian Education, 7.2.95.

....A survey in Birmingham in 1991 found that as many as three quarters of school children there were working in some capacity. The Low Pay Unit estimates that up to two million children in the UK do part-time work -- the worst record in Europe.

On June 22 1994 the European Directive on child labour was approved by the European parliament. This legislation allows any child to work a maximum of 12 hours a week, and totally bans night working.

But the British government opposed the European legislation, saying that it might damage the competitiveness of British business and negotiated exemptions from the treaty. This means that the new rules for 16- to 18-year olds, which limit both hours worked and night working, will not be law in the UK for another four years.

A similar approach towards child labour, also led by economic considerations, is taken in India. Industries that employ child labour stay "competitive" because they pay lower wages to children than adults. Their production costs are therefore lower and they are able to sell their products at a cheaper price. Children as young as six are being forced to work for more than 12 hours a day on looms, producing carpets for European and US customers. They often sleep next to the looms and, if injured at work, may be treated with diesel oil to stem the blood flow and stop it staining the carpets....

# Should child labour be banned?

Role play cards

### Factory owner

You think children make the best loom workers. They've got small hands and nimble fingers, not to mention good eyesight. And this way you keep your costs down and make a profit. The law allows weaving "within the family" so you can just pretend the kids are relatives of yours!

### Child labourer

Carpet-making is long, hard work. It's hot, dusty and dark and you can easily get injured. If your work is not good enough you get punished. You've been here since you were 7 years old and you hate it. You think child labour should stop, but there needs to be help for all the children like you already working, many of them a long way from home.

### Parent

Your family needs the money your child earns. You yourself have no skills, and even if you did there is no work available. How are you supposed to live? You know it's a harsh way of life, but you think it is necessary. You believe that it's not good enough just to ban child labour without having other things in place first, like jobs for adults.

### Campaigner

You and your organisation are strongly opposed to child labour. It has a terrible effect on the children's health, and robs them of the chance for education. Employing adults may be more expensive but it is much better for the country in the long run. You are trying to start a scheme to give a special label to carpets produced without child labour.

### Indian government official

It is illegal under Indian law for children below the age of 15 to work, though you know that it goes on. But if you crack down here, the problem will probably just shift elsewhere in the region, and of course your industries must be competitive. Don't forget that plenty of child working goes on in Europe and North America too!

### US Senator

You think that adult workers in the United States should not have their jobs put at risk by these kinds of unfair and immoral practices. You believe that American customers also would rather not buy products made in this way. You are supporting a bill in Congress to ban all products made with child labour from entering the US.

# SECTION B:
## THE TRANSNATIONAL ECONOMY

### KEY IDEAS

4.3  The international mobility of capital is a key feature of the global economy. Multinational companies (MNCs) play a central role in this process.

4.4  MNCs, through the large size of their operations, have considerable influence on production and consumption in both the North and the South.

4.5  Industrial production has spread to many parts of the South, but has not benefited the majority of people there (eg. MNCs' use of Export Processing Zones).

4.6  In agricultural production, a small number of MNCs engaged in "agribusiness" increasingly control land and food worldwide.

### BACKGROUND

The world is becoming increasingly homogenised, with the same films, soft drinks, clothing and so on found all over the globe. Satellite communications enable advertising to penetrate almost any village. What are the effects of this on small local producers? on consumers? on cultural diversity?

A further issue is the question of MNCs' accountability compared to their power. Shareholders may take precedence over the interests of workers or the environment. How can companies which operate across so many borders be regulated effectively?

Students may ask why MNCs and Export Processing or Free Trade Zones are so heavily encouraged, through tax incentives and other means, by many governments when there are so many apparent disadvantages to them. It will be useful to help students make the links to earlier themes such as neocolonialism (Book 2), particularly the pressure of Structural Adjustment Programmes forcing countries to concentrate on increasing export earnings at the expense of social welfare spending.

We should not give the impression that governments are powerless in relation to MNCs. In Zambia, for instance, the copper mines which had been developed and run by the MNC Anglo-American were nationalised by the government in the early 1970s. In Botswana, the government has worked increasingly in partnership with South African mining MNCs to develop the country's mineral wealth. In both instances the respective governments have gained a greater proportion of the wealth generated through mining, and there are many more local people now in managerial positions.

Countries vary, however, in their capacity and readiness to stand up to MNCs and negotiate a better deal from them. There is an inevitable tension within "host" governments between preventing exploitation and driving such a hard (or fair?) bargain that companies move their operations elsewhere.

## SUGGESTED ACTIVITIES

The symbol ✪ on students' pages indicates more challenging tasks or questions, suitable for more able students.

**Page 24** Students could gather labels of these and other Unilever products and bring them in from home to create a display.

**Page 26** This page aims to help students grasp the sheer size of the largest MNCs. The statistics can be copied, cut up and handed out, one card per student (with extra pairs or full sets as needed for the size of the class, including some of the countries at the top of page 27 as "singles"). Students then walk around to find a "match" — ie. those with a country/GNP card must find someone with a company card showing sales of a similar size (say, within $6 billion). The six additional countries will not come anywhere near having a match, which should reinforce the point of the MNCs' relative size and influence.

**Page 29** How might citizens of "Exportania" feel about their government's offers? Students could take on the role of an Exportanian and write a letter to the President/Prime Minister to express those feelings.

**Pages 30 to 37** Any of the examples could be used as a basis for asking students to decide in groups what they would do if they were the workers involved. Do any of the students come up with the idea of a union? What obstacles might be involved? For example, in some countries when unions attempt to organise, companies close down, fire the workers and then reopen nearby with non-unionised labour; union organisers may suffer severe repression.

**Page 35** Can students think of any local examples of the effects of a factory or other big employer closing down?

**Page 36** More able students could try to come up with the company's needs and desirable product characteristics without seeing the table. As a related practical task, students could go to a supermarket or greengrocer's near closing time to see which kinds of items have been rejected by shoppers (bruised, blemished etc.). Perhaps they could arrange to interview a shopkeeper about what qualities the shoppers seem to look for; and then consider the implications for food suppliers.

**Page 38** A combined class list of questions could be drawn up, to be debated and decided by a chosen "government panel".

# Multinational corporations

? How many of the brands below do you recognise?

 Draw lines to match the names with the type of product.

Batchelors
Birds Eye
Brooke Bond
Flora
Lifebuoy
Lipton
Pears
Persil
Signal
Stork
Surf
Timotei

! ALL of these products (and many more) are made by a single large company: Unilever. It has been estimated that two-thirds of the world's people come across Unilever products every day of their lives.

 Refer to the exercise above. Which types of product above have more than one Unilever brand?

Type of product      Brands

✺ Why would one company want to produce several brands of the same thing?

24.... BOOK 4 -- PRODUCTION AND ITS EFFECTS

* Unilever is an example of a **multinational** or **transnational** corporation (MNC or TNC — both terms are used). An MNC or TNC, as the names suggest, operates in many (**multi**) countries or across (**trans**) national boundaries.

* By the early 1990s, there were an estimated 37,000 MNCs, 24,000 of them based in 14 major industrialised countries. MNCs with headquarters in the South make up only 8% of the total. According to the United Nations, MNCs now control 70 per cent of world trade.

Find words from the box at the bottom to fill in the gaps in the description of MNCs below.

MNCs are companies which have their _____ in one country but have _____ or _____ in other countries. They have the ability to cross national _____ in search of lower _____ -- like cheap labour and natural _____ -- in order to make higher _____. This means that MNCs, particularly in dangerous and dirty _____, tend to move to countries which have lower environmental _____ and fewer _____ about workers' pay and conditions.

**borders   branches   costs   factories   headquarters**
**industries   profits   resources   rules   standards**

! US trade magazine Chemical Week has reported that US chemical firms spend 44% less on pollution control at their overseas plants than at those inside the country.

What reasons can you suggest for the difference in spending?

# MNCs: Size and influence

MNCs, through their size and spread around the world, have great influence on what goods are produced and consumed in both North and South.

**?** Just how big are the biggest MNCs? Compare the sales of the MNCs below with the size of the entire national economy of selected countries.

| | |
|---|---|
| **General Motors** (Motor vehicles/parts; USA) Sales: $123.7 billion | **Taiwan** GNP: $129.5 billion |
| **Royal Dutch/Shell** (Petroleum refining; Netherlands/UK) Sales: $103.8 billion | **Indonesia** GNP: $109.0 billion |
| **IBM** (Computers/office equipment; USA) Sales: $65.3 billion | **Thailand** GNP: $67.6 billion |
| **Philip Morris** (Food and tobacco; USA) Sales: $48.1 billion | **Philippines** GNP: $42.7 billion |
| **Du Pont** (Chemicals; USA) Sales: $38.0 billion | **Egypt** GNP: $34.0 billion |
| **Boeing** (Aerospace; USA) Sales: $29.3 billion | **Chile** GNP: $25.6 billion |
| **Procter & Gamble** (Soaps/cosmetics; USA) Sales: $27.4 billion | **Bangladesh** GNP: $24.3 billion |
| **PepsiCo** (Beverages; USA) Sales: $19.7 billion | **Peru** GNP: $22.0 billion |

Source for company data: *New Internationalist*, August 1993.

Source for country data: *Third World Guide 1993-94*.

## Additional country cards

| Kenya<br>GNP: $9.4 billion | Tanzania<br>GNP: $3.6 billion |
|---|---|
| Guatemala<br>GNP: $8.1 billion | Malawi<br>GNP: $1.5 billion |
| Ethiopia<br>GNP: $5.6 billion | Chad<br>GNP: $1.1 billion |

Source for country data: *Third World Guide 1993-94*.

❂ Choose one of the following and explain what you think it means. You may need some knowledge of colonialism to tackle the second one.

> ❝ If multinationals had their way, the whole world would consume the same things. ❞
>
> *New Internationalist*, June 1987.
>
> (Hint: Why might MNCs like it if people everywhere ate, drank, wore or used the same goods? Think about the costs of producing goods, advertising them etc.)

> ❝ By developing products that can be produced anywhere and sold everywhere... by connecting global channels of communication that can penetrate any village or neighbourhood, these institutions... are becoming the world empires of the 21st century. ❞
>
> *Third World Resurgence* no. 40.

B) The transnational economy ....27

# Industrialisation: who wins, who loses?

In India, Gandhi developed a set of principles about village industry.

✏️ Try to think of an example to fit each principle and write it in the space provided.

The best kind of industry is that which uses the resources of the local area itself to produce things that help local people.

The next best is one which uses outside raw materials for things that help people in the village.

Third comes those which use local raw materials for things that are sold outside the area.

And worst are those industries which bring in outside raw materials, process them using village labour, and then export the products.

# MNCs and Export Processing Zones

Many Southern countries rely heavily on agriculture, but there has also been rapid growth in industry, especially for export. "Host" governments often promise companies many benefits to come and set up factories.

 Read the letter and use a highlighter pen to mark the features that might appeal to an MNC thinking about investing in a new location.

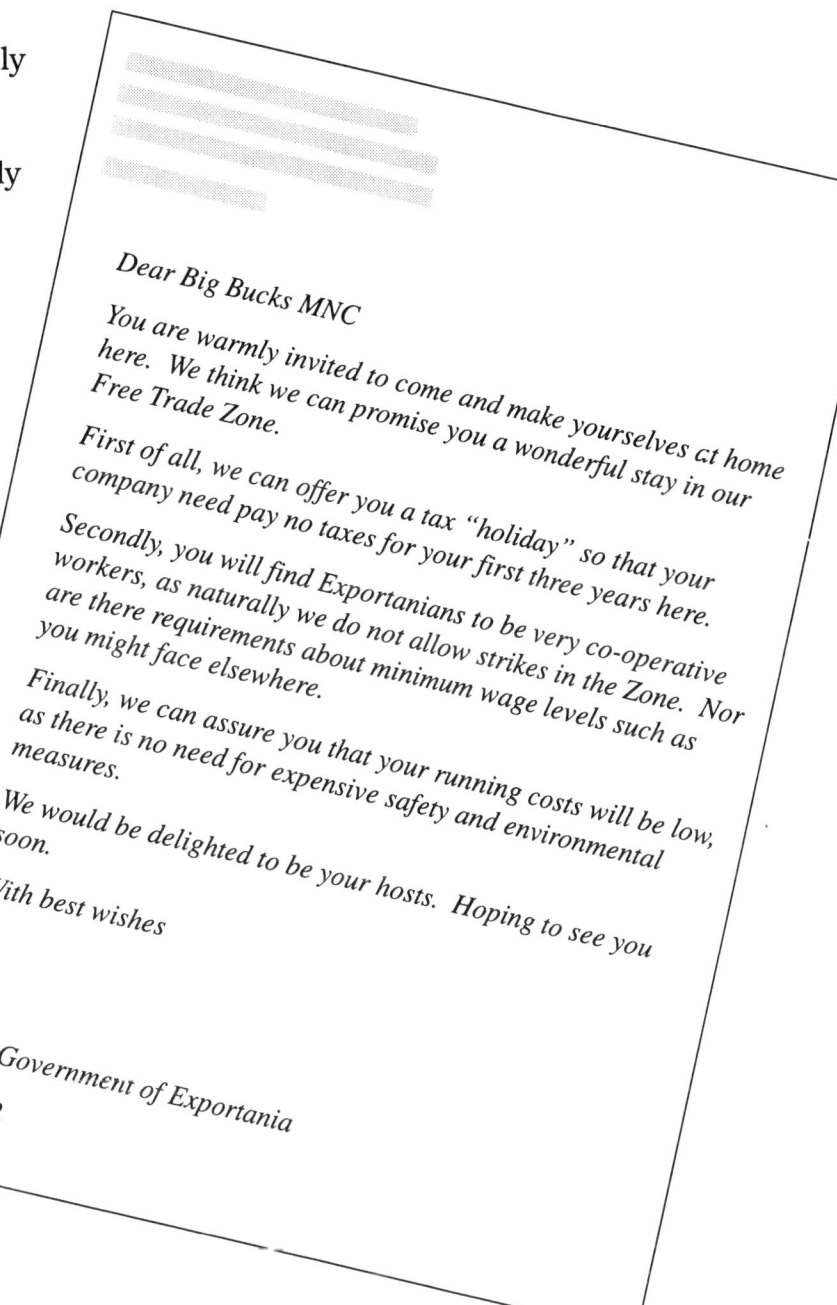

Dear Big Bucks MNC

You are warmly invited to come and make yourselves at home here. We think we can promise you a wonderful stay in our Free Trade Zone.

First of all, we can offer you a tax "holiday" so that your company need pay no taxes for your first three years here.

Secondly, you will find Exportanians to be very co-operative workers, as naturally we do not allow strikes in the Zone. Nor are there requirements about minimum wage levels such as you might face elsewhere.

Finally, we can assure you that your running costs will be low, as there is no need for expensive safety and environmental measures.

We would be delighted to be your hosts. Hoping to see you soon.

With best wishes

The Government of Exportania
RSVP.

Many MNCs have accepted the invitation to set up shop in the South, especially in **Export Processing Zones** (EPZs). There are now an estimated 260 such zones in 67 countries, where workers use materials shipped in to them to put together toys, clothing, electronic goods and so on. Then the finished products are sent away again for sale overseas.

 How do EPZs compare with Gandhi's principles about village industry (see page 28)?

B) The transnational economy ....29

# Case study: Nike

Source A

### THE NEW YORK TIMES, FEBRUARY 13, 1994
## Just Undo It: Nike's Exploited Workers

By RICHARD J. BARNET
and JOHN CAVANAGH

.... The Indonesian girls and young women who sew the shoes start at an entry-level rate of $1.35 a day. (Michael Jordan's reported $20 million fee for promoting Nikes in 1992 exceeded the entire annual payroll of the Indonesian factories that make the shoes.) Overtime is often mandatory, and union protections are nearly nonexistent. If there is a strike, the military often will break it up.

Nike and its contractors are in the business of chasing such cheap labor. In the last five years, as wages have risen, they have closed down 20 production sites in South Korea and Taiwan and opened up new ones in China, Indonesia and Thailand, where wages are rock-bottom.

Source B

### EASTERN EXPRESS, MAY 1, 1994
## Nike trips up on workers' rights

Jan Alexander

.... Deborah Leipziger, a researcher at CEP [Council on Economic Priorities], says employees at two factories in the Jakarta area, mostly women, work as much as 12 hours a day and live in barracks which they can leave only on Sunday with written permission from management.

Source C

### BBC WORLDWIDE | October 1994

.... Young women work long hours in noisy factories making Nike shoes for subcontractors from Taiwan and South Korea. It is true, as Nike says, that most of them are earning the legal minimum wage. But then by the Indonesian Government's own admission, the minimum wage (3,800 rupiah or about $1.80 per day) is not enough to fulfil a single adult's basic minimum needs.

Source D

**LOS ANGELES TIMES, DECEMBER 12, 1994**

## Relief Elusive for Asia's Labor Pains

.... "Companies like Nike can put a pair of $150 shoes on the docks with only 35 or 40 cents of labor," said Charles Gray, head of international affairs for the AFL-CIO [American Federation of Labor and Congress of Industrial Organizations] in Washington. "I think that's criminal almost. Certainly greedy."

Source for all clippings: *Nike in Indonesia Newsletter*, Press for Change, Inc., February 1995.

Use the sources to answer the questions below. (The letters in brackets indicate which sources you will need.)

1. In what countries has Nike closed down plants in the last 5 years? (A)

2. In what countries has Nike opened plants? Why? (A)

3. Complete the bar graph. (A, C)

4. What are the labour costs for a pair of Nike shoes? (D)

5. How much does a pair of Nikes sell for in the United States? (D)

Describe working conditions inside the Indonesian factories. (A, B, C)

B) The transnational economy ....31

# Case study: Clothing export factories

## Honduras

A former worker in a garment assembly plant has described the conditions there as follows:

"While we work, the supervisors yell, "Hurry up, hurry up", and hit us on the forehead. If an operator is unable to complete a task quickly, a manager will grab her by the back of the head and smash her against the sewing machines."

There are eight toilets for 900 people. Working hours are from 7.30 am until at least 6.30 pm. After women have worked at the factory for two months, they are forced to take a pregnancy test. If the test is positive, the worker is fired.

*News from IRENE,* September 1994.

## Sri Lanka

"Export garment factories employ mostly rural, unmarried women between the ages of 16-25 years. Since they are paid very low, they live in the cheapest possible lodgings, sharing a small house with a number of other working girls.

"The very low-quality cheap food they eat, which they cook only once for the whole day, has created very high rates of malnutrition among these workers. They travel in extremely crowded buses.

"The availability of cheap labour in such large numbers has allowed the factory owners to keep the workers in conditions of no job security, with very low wages and poor facilities."

DP Rodrigo and MS Jayasinghe,
Uva Community Development Centre, Pasarra, Sri Lanka (AMIHAN, 1993).

**?** Why might factories prefer to employ mainly young, unmarried women?

When conditions in the factories are so bad, why do you think people agree to work there?

Choose one of the above accounts and use it to write a diary entry from the point of view of a factory worker.

# Health and safety

### India

On December 3, 1984, Bhopal in India was devastated by an explosion at the US-owned Union Carbide pesticide factory. The explosion spread clouds of poisonous gases that killed thousands and injured countless more. Most of the victims are still waiting for compensation.

In a report to Union Carbide's Chief Executive Officer, the Bhopal Medical Commission wrote:

"We feel it is our duty to let you know of our astonishment at the disregard your company has shown for the rights of the people of Bhopal. It is our firm belief that most of the accepted standards of industrial accident prevention and safety have been grossly violated."

Source: International Medical Appeal for Bhopal, December 1994.

### Thailand and China

May 1993: 210 people, mainly women, died in a factory near Bangkok, Thailand.

November 1993: 81 people died in a factory in China's "special economic zone" of Shenzhen.

Both factories were making toys for export. In both cases, basic safety standards were lacking: doors were locked to prevent theft and absence.

List any common elements you can find in the Bhopal, Bangkok and Shenzhen cases.

  What do you think should be done about such cases, and by whom?

What difficulties might there be in trying to control companies which are foreign-owned and run?

B) The transnational economy ....33

# Environmental impact

### Mexico

Along the Rio Grande border with the United States, multinational companies have taken advantage of rock-bottom wages (the equivalent of 35p an hour in one television plant) and lack of laws about the environment and workers' rights to set up nearly 1,800 export-only factories -- so-called **maquiladoras** -- employing half a million workers.

The result, according to Susan George, a director of the Transnational Institute, a development think-tank, is a "disaster zone". Border towns have been turned into toxic dumps, rivers flow with dangerous waste, sewage routinely contaminates drinking water. "For ordinary people," Ms George says, "crowded and unsanitary living conditions and environmental destruction have combined to make the maquiladora zone... hell on earth."

*Independent on Sunday,* 12.12.93.

Find words from the article to fit the definitions below.

equal to _____

Mexican export-only factories _____

same as multinational _____

poisonous _____

pollutes _____

dirty or unhealthy _____

Design a poster about the environmental effects of the maquiladoras.

34.... BOOK 4 -- PRODUCTION AND ITS EFFECTS

# When MNCs move

### Canada

Bendix, part of a huge American-owned corporation which manufactures everything from oil filters to industrial solvents, recently closed down a plant in Ontario, Canada. Work was shifted to plants in the US and Mexico.

"We were angry when they told us the plant would be closed. There were no good reasons; they were making money. It doesn't hit home until it happens to you -- you feel so powerless. Your world is suddenly turned upside down and there's nothing you can do to stop it."

Alice, 38 years old, employee of Bendix for 19 years.

"The company used to tell us this was the most productive plant in the system, but quality didn't mean anything in the final decision. We had decent wages and a good pension plan; that was the problem as far as the company was concerned. Why not go south where labour costs are cheaper? Companies like Bendix can close and they don't have to justify the decision to anyone. They just can't be allowed to disrupt people's lives like they do when the decision is based only on maximising profit."

Al Seymour, 52 years old, Canadian Auto Workers Union.

Source: *New Internationalist,* August 1993.

1. Choose 2 words from Alice's statement which show how she felt about the plant closing down.

2. What did Al Seymour like about working for Bendix?

3. How productive was the Ontario plant compared with others?

4. Why did the company move?

 Who else besides the people who actually worked in the factory could suffer from its closing? What might be the effects on the rest of the community/ town?

# MNCs and food

A small number of MNCs engaged in **agribusiness** -- large-scale, commercial agricultural production -- increasingly control land and food worldwide.

5 companies control 77% of the cereals trade worldwide.
3 companies control 80% of the banana trade.
3 companies control 83% of the cocoa trade.
3 companies control 85% of the tea trade.
4 companies control 87% of the tobacco trade.

Source: *Raw Deal.*

| Type of crop | | | | | |
|---|---|---|---|---|---|
| Share of trade | | | | | |
| Controlled by how many companies | | | | | |

What kinds of methods/products would be favoured by a giant food company? Imagine, for example, a firm selling bananas round the world.

✏ Choose from the phrases given at the bottom to complete the table.

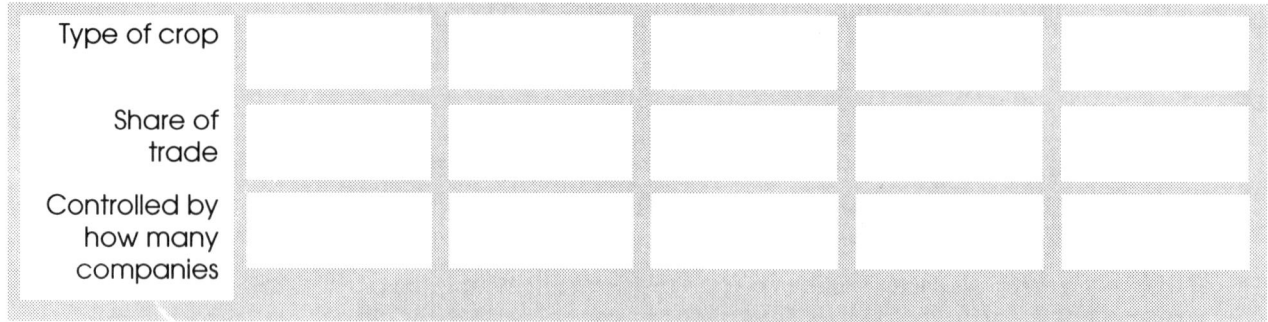

| | Needs of the company | Desired qualities of fruit |
|---|---|---|
| 1 | | thick peel, uniform shape |
| 2 | ship large quantity all at once | |
| 3 | | does not go off too quickly |
| 4 | attract customers in the shops | |

> transport over long times and distances,  free from marks or blemishes,
> pack tightly together for shipping,  all the fruit ripens at the same time.

✺ Agribusiness MNCs have changed the qualities of fruit and vegetables to suit their own needs. Why might a small-scale farmer prefer a crop which ripens a small amount at a time?

36.... BOOK 4 -- PRODUCTION AND ITS EFFECTS

# Bananas

Dole, part of the US food giant Castle and Cooke, runs banana farms on Mindanao island in the Philippines.

*Choose words from the box at the bottom to fill in the gaps.*

"The bananas here are better loved and _____ for than the workers," says Connie Actub, health and safety officer with the National Federation of Labour. "Every possible step is _____ to keep the _____ fruits from suffering the slightest bruise," she says. "That is hardly how the workers are _____."

A 1984 Philippines Labour Ministry study _____ that the banana sector consumes 80 per cent of the herbicides and 90 per cent of the fungicides used in the country. Banana plantations are also _____ by the Government to apply hazardous pesticides such as Paraquat which are not permitted on other crops. This shows up in the packing plants.

"All the chemicals _____ in the field end up in here. Freshly harvested bananas are first _____ in large water tanks to wash off the chemicals. Many workers who handle the bananas in these tanks find their fingernails become _____ — or even fall off," says Yolanda Martinez, a supervisor in the packing plant. Very little protective clothing or safety advice is _____.

Source: *New Internationalist*, November 1991.

---

**allowed, cared, discoloured, harvested, placed
provided, showed, taken, treated, used**

B) The transnational economy ....37

✏️ List five things shown in the cartoon which would make "Silver Coast" a bad place to work.

1

2

3

4

5

☀ After what you have learned about MNCs, what questions would you want to ask before allowing MNCs to operate in your country? List them below.

# SECTION C:
## MIGRATION AND URBANISATION

### KEY IDEAS

4.7 Increasing poverty, landlessness and lack of livelihood in rural areas can push people to leave and try to find employment in urban areas (or in other countries).

4.8 Cities are often unable to accommodate all those seeking jobs. Many people end up trying to make a living in the "informal economy".

4.9 The pressures of migration and urban life have tended to undermine traditional family patterns and ways of life in the South.

### BACKGROUND

It has been estimated that some 20 million people move from the countryside to cities every year. Section C examines the reasons for the phenomenon of urban growth, which is particularly evident in the South, and its impact on both individuals and cities. Students are encouraged to identify the factors which may push or pull people towards the city, and to compare migrants' hopes with urban realities. The differences beween the formal and informal economy are explored, as well as the question of how migration and urbanisation affect extended families.

### SUGGESTED ACTIVITIES

The symbol ✪ on students' pages indicates more challenging tasks or questions, suitable for more able students.

**Page 41** The true/false exercise could be used twice, once before starting the topic to see what students already know or think, and again after the topic has been covered.

**Pages 42-43** To extend the activity, students can use an atlas and work in pairs to plot the 21 largest cities onto a blank world map. (The North-South map provided on page 20, Book 1, would be ideal.) What do they notice about the distribution of these cities?

**Pages 44-46** You could start by asking for a show of hands of any students who have moved house, and ask volunteers to state the reasons. (Be aware of possible upset amongst those whose families have experienced divorce, refugee situations etc.) Students could then broaden this into a brainstorm of reasons why people might move specifically from villages to cities, before looking at the push and pull factors given on pages 44 and 45 (adapted from *The Gaia Atlas of Cities* and *New Internationalist*). The cards can be copied and cut up, with students in pairs sorting them into "push" or "pull". For more of a challenge, the headings could be cut off, to be matched with the explanations before sorting. For less able students, pages 44 and 45 could be reproduced without being cut up, and the information transferred directly onto the table, page 46.

**Pages 48-49** You will need one copy of the double-page game "board" (copied straight onto A3 if possible, or stuck onto A3 backing) for each group of 2 to 4 players, and dice for determining moves (one die per group). Each player needs some small marker as a piece to move round the board. The first player to reach the city wins. It is essential to follow up the learning points of the game with page 50.

**Page 51** To illustrate the point about overcrowding, a class average of room density could be compiled, using the number of rooms per household divided by the number of people who live there. (This will need sensitive handling depending on the housing conditions of your students.) It should also be noted that Western notions of the need for privacy and "personal space" are not universally shared.

**Page 53** The two case studies come from *New Internationalist*, July 1987 and April 1989.

**Page 55** Copy and cut up enough sets of cards for pair or small group work. After students read page 54, ask them to sort the cards into "formal" and "informal".

**Page 56** Can students guess the effect of urbanisation on average household size?

# Migration and urbanisation

*Mark the following statements T (true) or F (false). Then rewrite any false statements to make them true.*

1. Most of the world's 10 largest cities are found in Europe and North America.

2. Worldwide, about 20 million people move from the countryside to cities each year.

3. Lack of land is an important factor forcing people to leave their villages.

4. Cities generally have no problem absorbing all those who wish to live and work there.

5. A "shantytown" is a planned settlement providing basic services such as power, water and sanitation.

6. Official jobs with taxed salaries are part of the "informal" economy.

7. Most urban jobs in countries of the South are in the "formal" economy.

8. City life tends to favour smaller families.

# An increasingly urban world

! In 1950, only two cities -- London and New York -- had populations of more than 8 million.

Compare that with the figures for 1990:

| City | Population in millions |
|---|---|
| Beijing | 10.8 |
| Bombay | 11.2 |
| Buenos Aires | 11.5 |
| Cairo | 9.0 |
| Calcutta | 11.8 |
| Delhi | 8.8 |
| Jakarta | 9.3 |
| London | 10.4 |
| Los Angeles | 11.9 |
| Manila | 8.5 |
| Mexico City | 20.2 |
| Moscow | 8.8 |
| New York | 16.2 |
| Osaka | 8.5 |
| Paris | 8.5 |
| Rio de Janeiro | 10.7 |
| Sao Paulo | 17.4 |
| Seoul | 11.0 |
| Shanghai | 13.4 |
| Tianjin | 9.4 |
| Tokyo/Yokohama | 23.4 |

Source: *The Gaia Atlas of Cities,* 1992.

✎ Rearrange the information from page 42 to fill in the table of cities, starting with the city having the highest population as number 1. You may need to refer to an atlas to complete the last two columns.

|    | Name of city | Population (millions) | Country | Continent |
|----|---|---|---|---|
| 1  |   |   |   |   |
| 2  |   |   |   |   |
| 3  |   |   |   |   |
| 4  |   |   |   |   |
| 5  |   |   |   |   |
| 6  |   |   |   |   |
| 7  |   |   |   |   |
| 8  |   |   |   |   |
| 9  |   |   |   |   |
| 10 |   |   |   |   |
| 11 |   |   |   |   |
| 12 |   |   |   |   |
| 13 |   |   |   |   |
| 14 |   |   |   |   |
| 15 |   |   |   |   |
| 16 |   |   |   |   |
| 17 |   |   |   |   |
| 18 |   |   |   |   |
| 19 |   |   |   |   |
| 20 |   |   |   |   |
| 21 |   |   |   |   |

✪ "Urban growth, a trend that started in Europe and North America, is now centred on the South." What evidence can you find to support this statement?

C) Migration and urbanisation ....43

# Urbanisation: "push" and "pull" factors

It has been estimated that some 20 million people move from the countryside to cities every year.

**?** What forces them to leave their village, or attracts them towards the city?

## Push factors

| | |
|---|---|
| **NO LAND** | Many people do not have a big enough, or fertile enough, piece of land to grow their own food and support themselves. On a small plot, the soil can wear out through being over-worked. Also, export crops favour big farmers who can afford machines, fertilisers and high-yield seeds. Small farmers may lose their land and have to look for work in the city. |
| **NO WORK** | Governments tend to support city-based industries while ignoring rural areas. Local economic decline can drive young people from the villages to seek opportunities for employment, education and advancement elsewhere. |
| **DISASTERS** | Wars, droughts, floods and other disasters may force people into refugee camps which are often on the outskirts of major cities. |
| **COUNTRY BLUES** | The countryside may be seen as backward and dull, an image now common with the global spread of consumer culture. Young people may feel there is nothing to do in their village and no reason to stay. |

**Pull factors**

| BRIGHT LIGHTS and FREEDOM | Cities appear more exciting and glamorous; they attract the bored, the lonely, the ambitious and the adventurous. Money, comfort and amusement beckon. Young people who feel hemmed in by tradition and rigid customs come to lose themselves in the crowds. |
|---|---|
| WORK | Wages are higher and jobs seem more plentiful in the city. Living costs are higher too but the possibility of paid work is a powerful draw. |
| BETTER LIVING | City dwellers may end up in slums but they are usually closer to clinics and hospitals and probably have easier access to electricity and water than in the countryside. |
| EVERYONE ELSE IS DOING IT | Some people may want to head for the city to join family or friends who have gone before. |

C) Migration and urbanisation ....45

Use the information from pages 44 and 45 to fill in the table. Explain each factor briefly in your own words.

| Push factors | Pull factors |
|---|---|
| 1 | 1 |
| 2 | 2 |
| 3 | 3 |
| 4 | 4 |

# Will you make it in the city?

> **"** We asked for workers, but human beings came. **"**
> Max Frisch, Swiss writer.

You have arrived in the city with no money, no job, no relatives there.

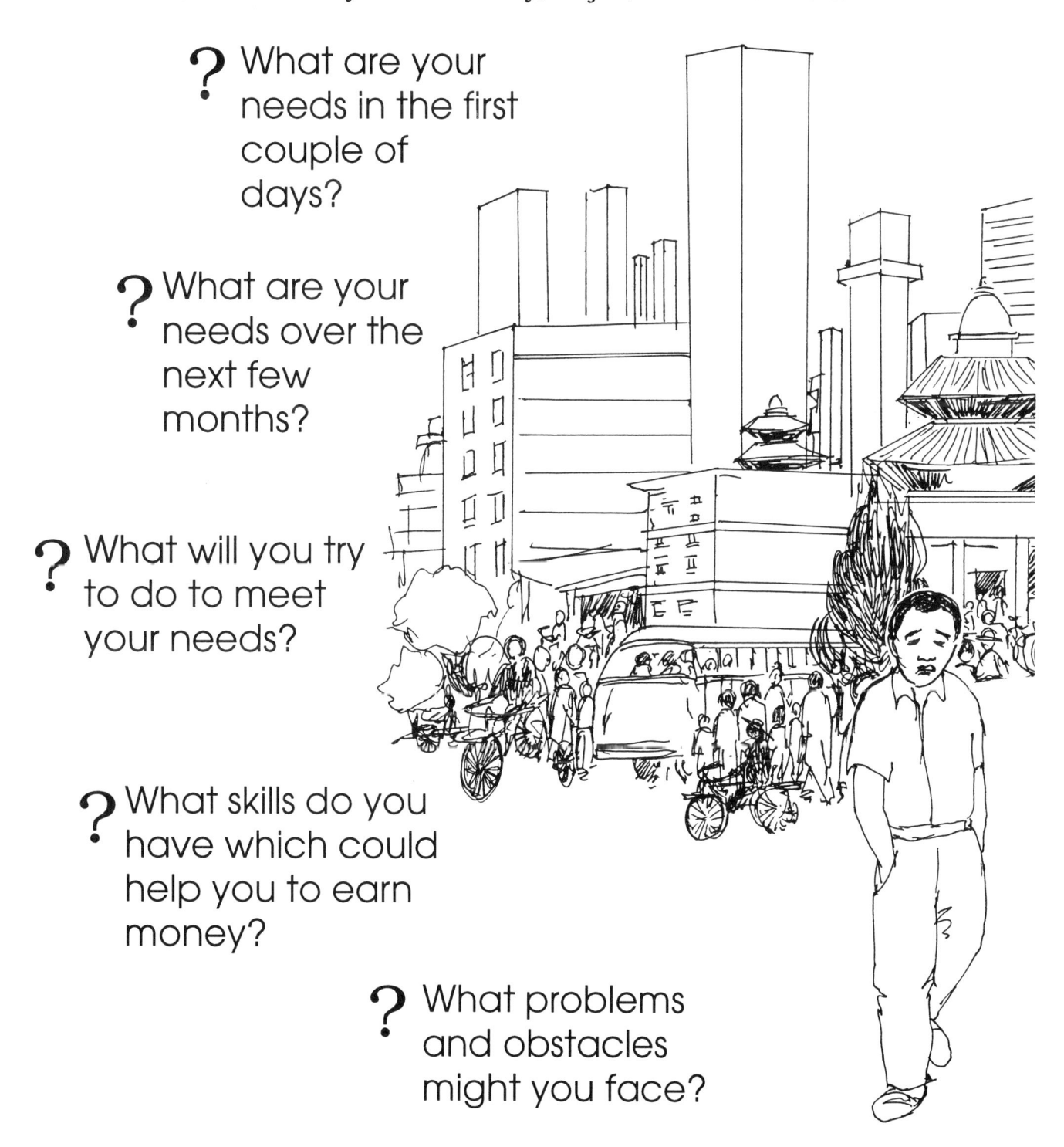

**?** What are your needs in the first couple of days?

**?** What are your needs over the next few months?

**?** What will you try to do to meet your needs?

**?** What skills do you have which could help you to earn money?

**?** What problems and obstacles might you face?

C) Migration and urbanisation ....47

# City challenge

A game for 2-4 players

Take turns to roll the dice and move your marker the right number of spaces. When you land on a space with writing in it, the group must decide together whether you should move forward or back.

* If the writing says something which you all agree will **help** you survive in the city, move **forward** the number of spaces you are told. (The spaces with arrows in them count as well.)

* If the writing says something which you all agree will **harm** your chances of survival, move **back** the number of spaces you are told.

When you land on a space with arrows in it, you must wait there until your next turn. The first player to reach the city wins.

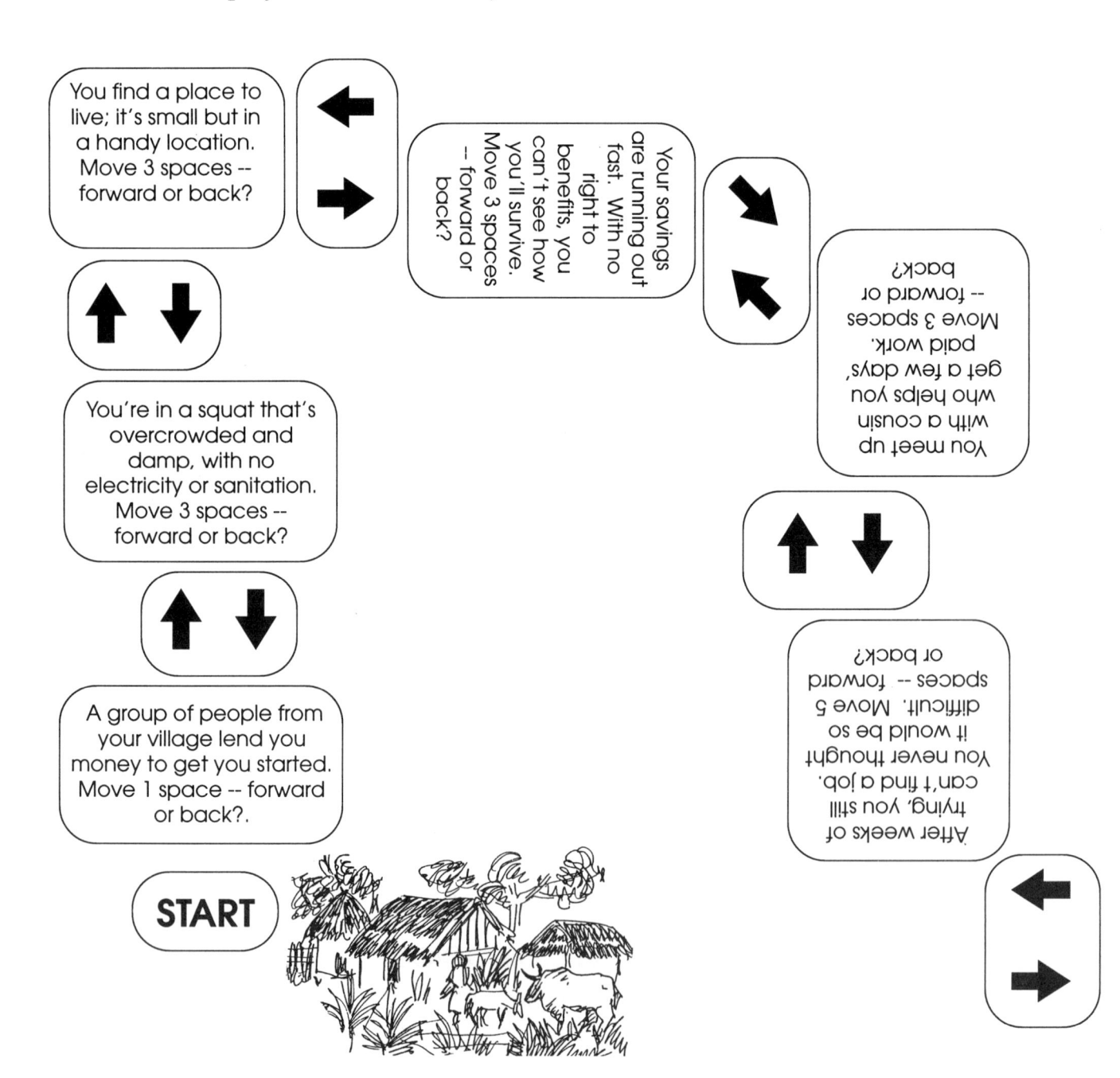

- You find a place to live; it's small but in a handy location. Move 3 spaces -- forward or back?

- Your savings are running out fast. With no right to benefits, you can't see how you'll survive. Move 3 spaces -- forward or back?

- You meet up with a cousin who helps you get a few days' paid work. Move 3 spaces -- forward or back?

- You're in a squat that's overcrowded and damp, with no electricity or sanitation. Move 3 spaces -- forward or back?

- A group of people from your village lend you money to get you started. Move 1 space -- forward or back?.

- After weeks of trying, you still can't find a job. You never thought it would be so difficult. Move 5 spaces -- forward or back?

START

48.... BOOK 4 -- PRODUCTION AND ITS EFFECTS

You set up a successful food stall, making and selling hot snacks. Move 1 space -- forward or back?

You had a false idea of what the city would be like. Now you wish you'd never left home. Go back to the start.

You feel very lonely, missing all the friends and family you left behind. Move 1 space -- forward or back?

**FINISH**

Well done! You're one of the lucky ones. Looks like you have a good chance of surviving in the city.

You make some new friends, and begin to feel more at home in the city. Move 1 space -- forward or back?

You've been doing part-time work in a factory. Now you're sacked without warning. Move 3 spaces -- forward or back?

You work with others to improve the area where you live and get basic services. Move 5 spaces -- forward or back?

C) Migration and urbanisation ....49

# City challenge summary

✏️ Using the game board on pages 48 and 49 to help you, list six things which can help rural migrants survive in the city.

1
2
3
4
5
6

List six things which make urban life very difficult for migrants.

1
2
3
4
5
6

# Life in the city

Many people arrive in cities with high hopes, but what are conditions really like?

## Overcrowding

Overcrowding can be extreme in inner cities, mainly because it is vital for people to be as near as possible to any source of work.

**Some city densities (people per room):**

| | |
|---|---|
| Bombay, India | 4.2 |
| Guangzhou, China | 5.7 |
| Lagos, Nigeria | 5.8 |
| London, UK | 0.6 |
| New York, USA | 0.5 |

Source: *The Gaia Atlas of Cities*, 1992.

✏ Draw stick figures to show the level of crowding in the named cities below. The first one has been done for you.

| Bombay | Guangzhou | Lagos | London | New York |

## Lack of services

Jobless migrants to the city have little spare cash. In the South most end up living in unplanned settlements (sometimes called **shantytowns**). These usually lack water, sewers, rubbish removal, power, paved streets and other services like postal delivery and fire-fighting. They are located on the worst land, near swamps, rubbish tips, dirty industrial sites or on steep hillsides. Houses are cramped, living conditions dangerous and disease common.

## Lack of work

"The unemployed cannot remain idle, simply because they would then starve. What they do is to try to get some kind of casual employment. And that's why they live in the shanties, however uncomfortable these places may be. Because these are the places that are closest to the commercial centres where work may be available."

Ainsley Samarajiwa, community worker in a shanty settlement in Colombo, Sri Lanka.

✺ Imagine you've been in the city for several weeks now. Write a letter to a friend back in your village who's thinking of coming to join you, describing what it's really like.

C) Migration and urbanisation ....51

# Case study: China

## Source A

"Intent on escaping the poverty and unemployment of the countryside, tens of millions of Chinese villagers have flooded into the cities in search of the jobs and new opportunities promised by Deng Xiaoping's reforms. For some the arduous journey has secured employment and wages previously unimaginable; for others it has meant sweat-shop factory conditions, the squalor of urban unemployment or an empty-handed trek back home....

Migrants sit hopefully by the roadside with hand-made signs describing their skills.... These workers are in an administrative vacuum with no rights to housing, education or health care."

*Independent on Sunday*, 6.11.94

## Source B

"Wu Su-ching, 63, collects cardboard boxes for a living. For 15 years her home has been an insect-infested concrete staircase off a Kowloon backstreet. She sleeps on plywood boards on a first-floor landing. The same space is her living room, dining room and kitchen.... (It is) an improvement, says the husband, Chan Yin-shing, over the village they fled two decades ago in one of China's poorest provinces: 'Life here is a tiny bit better than in the countryside.'"

*The Guardian,* 28.10.95

1. Identify the push and pull factors mentioned in Source A.
   Push:                           Pull:

2. Using Sources A and B, list four problems faced by the migrants.

52.... BOOK 4 -- PRODUCTION AND ITS EFFECTS

# Case study: Peru

## Source A

**Marta** migrated to Lima from the Andean town of Huancayo with her parents.

"My father thought there would be more jobs in the capital. But things just got worse. Prices kept going up and my father couldn't get a job. He took to heavy drinking and then he took off with another woman. My seven younger brothers and I had to go to work to help our mother." She has become an **ambulante**, or roving seller, hawking cigarettes and chocolate bars along the main street in the Miraflores commercial district.

## Source B

**Victor** is an 11 year old in a shantytown on the south side of Lima, Peru. His mother has a potato stand on the market; he sells sweets.

"I started working when I was seven. I work because I've got to eat. Where I live, lots of kids work. For example, the little girl next door spends all her time at the bus-stop washing car windscreens. Others collect fares or sell candles. We help each other. Maybe if things were different we wouldn't have to work. But families can't survive unless their children earn money."

List five types of work done by rural migrants to Lima.

1
2
3
4
5

C) Migration and urbanisation ....53

# The informal economy

In the North, most people working away from the home have a fixed job in a fixed place, with an official job title. This kind of work makes up the **formal economy.**

In most Southern countries, those who can claim a steady job in a factory or office or government service are a privileged few. Everyone else makes a living as best they can, selling plates of food from roadside stalls, shining shoes, repairing cars on the pavement, or whatever else they can find to do. These people are working in the **informal economy.**

It is difficult to attach numbers to a phenomenon like this. But estimates in six Latin American and two Asian cities show that anywhere between 40 and 70 per cent of their urban workforces are "informal". These are in fact the workers who keep most cities going.

The way they make their living is strictly speaking illegal. This is rarely because they choose to break the law. Usually they just can't get into the official economy. Either they lack education, or money, or there simply aren't enough jobs.

| The formal economy | The informal economy |
|---|---|
| legal | illegal |
| taxes paid on money earned | no rights to social security benefits |
| written contracts | no official records |
| rules about health and safety | might include busking or casual building work |
| right to set up and belong to a union | also known as "underground" or "shadow" economy |

C) Migration and urbanisation ....55

# Family ties

**A** "There are men-only hostels in southern Africa located near centres of employment such as mines. A father goes there to find work, while the rest of the family is left behind depending on the money he sends back to them. In this way families and communities are divided."

Mercy Chikoti, Zambia.

**B** "In the village, you have your family and your neighbours -- you don't have to worry about tomorrow. Whatever happens, there are people who will help you and look after you. One of the big changes when you move to the city is that you do have to worry about tomorrow! You have to learn new skills to survive."

Ahmed El-Hassan, Sudan.

**C** "In the city, you keep up ties with the other people there from your village, like your **compadres** (godparents). You organise fiestas together just like before."

Martha Silver-Freire, Ecuador.

**D** "Migration from rural areas is changing the shape and behaviour of families. Family life in cities often requires a mobile and flexible workforce, not one tied down by an extended family. The cost of living is high, and it is expensive to educate children. It is hard to sustain large families."

*Families* (Gaia and UNESCO, 1993).

**E** "In Cameroon, people in the capital who come from the same tribe commonly gather in one person's house for a drink and discussions, for example, about how to pay the funeral expenses of the tribe's recently deceased members. These gatherings act as mutual self-help organisations.... As one resident says, 'You will find there are small villages that are carried into the cities. A town in Cameroon is a set of villages.'"

*New Scientist,* 7.10.95.

1  Which sources suggest that migration to cities causes extended families to break up?

2  Which ones suggest that family and village ties can be maintained?

# SECTION D:
## TECHNOLOGY AND SUSTAINABILITY

### KEY IDEAS

4.10 Technology which is researched and developed in one place is not necessarily right for other places. When introduced into the South, much Northern technology has proved unsuitable to the needs of its users and harmful to the environment.

4.11 Western concepts of land use and farming methods (eg. Green Revolution, large-scale farming, privatisation of common land), are seldom appropriate for the needs of the majority of farmers in the South.

4.12 Local problem-solving and technology which fits local needs and circumstances are key steps towards sustainable development.

### BACKGROUND

"Sustainability" has become a buzz word in the North — which is ironic, because many sustainable ways of life in the South have been destroyed through the imposition of Northern technology. Northern control of markets and information has also led to the denial or stifling of Southern creativity and knowledge, and the range of suitable indigenous technology which already exists.

When teaching about technology and sustainability, it is important to recognise and counter common assumptions such as those below (adapted from Intermediate Technology *Strategies and Guidelines* — see Recommended Resources):

> BIG IS BEST... HIGH TECH IS BETTER THAN LOW TECH... THE MORE IT COSTS, THE BETTER IT IS.... It is important to be sensitive to any connotations of "third rate for Third World". Small-scale technologies can appear to be "old-fashioned" and therefore "second-best" or "no good".

> DESIRABLE DEVELOPMENT MEANS BECOMING LIKE US. It is quite likely that pupils may think: WE are a Developed Country. THEY are a Less Developed Country. Therefore THEY need to

become more like US, with more of OUR technology.

The many environmental and other problems generated by "our" kind of technology should help to demonstrate that the North by no means has all the answers.

THEY'RE NOT AS CLEVER AS WE ARE. Scorn and patronising attitudes are common. Students should be encouraged to recognise the achievements of great Southern civilisations, past and present, and the determination of people and communities in the South to be self-reliant.

The Green Revolution is an excellent example of the potential pitfalls involved in technology, particularly when it is developed in one place and applied in another. (The information below, and on students' pages 64 and 65, is adapted from *New Internationalist*.)

Selective plant breeding has occurred since people first took up planting crops, in that they pick the best seeds for next year's planting. But harvest yields have stayed much the same. Some 20 years ago, however, research found new varieties of high-yielding seeds — wheat, maize and rice — which could double harvests. By 1985 Green Revolution seeds were being sown on half the acreage devoted to rice and wheat in the South.

In order to adopt the high yielding varieties (HYVs) with a good chance of success, farmers had to carry out all the weeding, watering, fertilising, transplanting, plant spacing and applying of pesticides, exactly as directed. They could not miss out any of the steps. HYVs made more demands on farmers than most traditional varieties which were adapted to give reasonable yields under poor or uncertain conditions, rather than high yields under the best possible conditions. Local growers also had to buy seeds, fertilisers, chemical products, machinery and fuel.

## SUGGESTED ACTIVITIES

The symbol ✪ on students' pages indicates more challenging tasks or questions, suitable for more able students.

**Page 63** Students could devise appropriate captions for the drawings.

**Pages 64-65** Students will need a brief introduction to what the Green Revolution was (see Background) before attempting the suggested activities.

The cards can be used in several ways. The two pages can be copied, cut up and mixed together for pairs or small groups to sort into positive and negative outcomes. Alternatively, all advantages cards can be given to half the groups, all disadvantages cards to the remaining groups; evaluations can then be presented and compared. A more challenging exercise is to give one card to each student, and ask them to walk around and find the "match" which balances out their own card (easier if advantages and disadvantages are copied onto two different colours). In all cases, after seeing/hearing both sides of the story, do students think the Green Revolution was good or bad on balance? For whom?

**Page 67** The apple example comes from Intermediate Technology *Strategies and Guidelines*. It can make a very effective and dramatic introduction to the topic of sustainability when the slicing, peeling etc. are actually carried out in front of students' eyes.

**Page 68** The cards are designed to be copied and cut up for a diamond ranking exercise: what do students consider the most important features of appropriate technology? For more of a challenge, the headings could be cut off and matched to the definitions before the ranking.

(Much work in this field is based on the ideas of EF Schumacher. Two key organisations currently working in this field are Intermediate Technology, based in Rugby, and the Centre for Alternative Technology, near Machynlleth, Powys. The characteristics listed on page 68 are adapted from material produced by these two groups.)

**Page 70** The Guri quote comes from *Bad Samaritans* by Paul Vallely (Hodder & Stoughton, 1990).

# What is technology?

**Technology** can be defined as the tools people use to meet their needs. It is about the practical use of knowledge to solve problems.

But technology can also create new problems.

✏️ Work with a partner to fill in the table below. The first example has been done for you.

| New technology | Problems solved | Problems created |
|---|---|---|
| machines in factories | faster, cheaper production | people out of work, pollution |
| cars | | |
| aerosol spray cans | | |
| computers | | |
| pesticides | | |
| asbestos | | |
| nuclear energy | | |

Can you add any other examples?

✺ Read the quote below. Do you agree or disagree? Give reasons for your answer.

> " No instrument, no skill, no crop introduced into a society from the outside is 'neutral'. No so-called technical solution for any problem remains technical longer than about five minutes. Any innovation is going to have far-reaching consequences on people's lives and will affect their jobs or lack of them, the direction their children will take, and how much they will or won't have to eat. "
>
> Susan George, *How the Other Half Dies.*

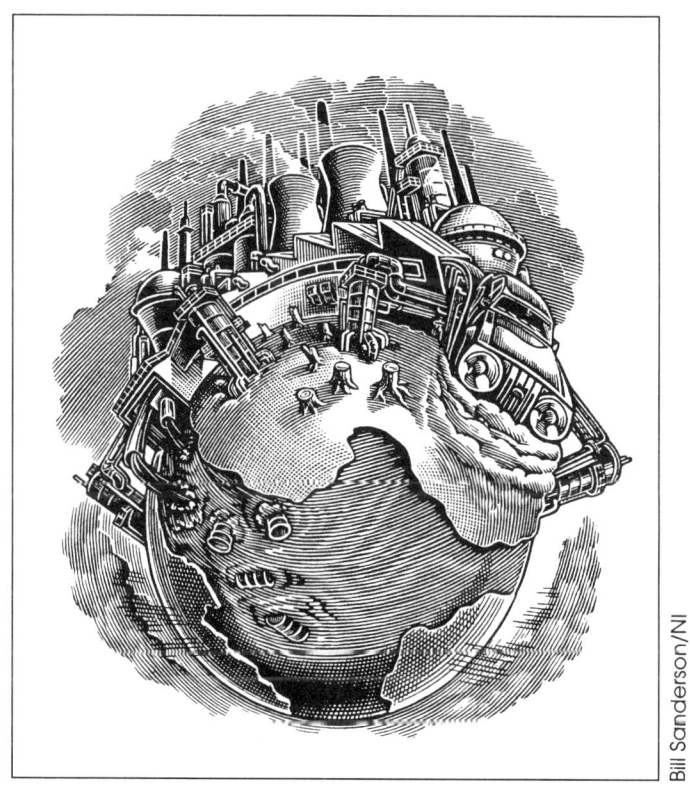

D) Technology and sustainability ....61

# The technology of food production

**?** How have farming and food production changed in Europe and North America over the past 50 years?

✎ Read the descriptions and draw a line to connect each one with the example that fits it best.

a — more **intensive** production of crops and rearing of livestock — in other words, producing more in the same space — based on greater use of fertilisers, chemicals and other inputs.

the decline in the traditional practice of crofting in Scotland

b — more **mechanised** production, resulting in a dramatic increase in the scale of holdings, the size of fields and the potential damage caused by cultivation.

the "Corn Belt": an area across several states in the US where nothing but corn is grown for miles on end

c — more **specialised** production, meaning a drop in the number of different types of crop produced in any one farm or region and a decline in mixed farming.

battery hens: keeping a large number of chickens in an enclosed space to increase egg production

d — more **concentrated** production in the most favourable and usually most fertile areas, associated with the abandonment of traditional farming in more difficult or less fertile areas.

the removal of hedgerows to create larger fields and allow tractors to be used more easily

1   What is the woman doing?  ⇨

2   What is the man doing?  ⇨

3   What advantages and disadvantages might there be in each style of farming?

⇦ 4   Who do you think the man is supposed to be?

⇦ 5   What is he offering to the woman?

6   What advantages and disadvantages might there be in accepting his offer?

Read the following quote and answer the questions.

> " In every village of Rajasthan you will find agricultural extension workers acting like drug pushers, trying to get every farmer onto chemicals by handing out free packets. "
>
> Srilata Swaminandhan, Indian activist.

1   What do you think the writer's attitude is towards the extension workers?

2   What kind of farming do you think the writer prefers?

D) Technology and sustainability ....63

# The Green Revolution

**?** Was the Green Revolution helpful or harmful? From whose point of view?

## Advantages

New high-yield varieties of seeds have been developed.

Bigger harvests since the Green Revolution have made far more food available in the world than before.

Farmers able to afford the investment can become very successful.

Countries such as India, Indonesia and Thailand have become self-sufficient in basic foodstuffs. They are no longer dependent on North American and European food aid.

Former food importers like India and Thailand now export grain, earning useful foreign currency.

New farming methods with irrigation can bring all-year-round employment. No longer must workers be laid off in the dry season.

Bigger harvests mean that the price of food stays constant or even falls in the marketplace, which helps consumers.

Green Revolution chemicals have helped to cut down on pests and produce bigger, healthier crops.

# Disadvantages

Traditional seed varieties, adapted over thousands of years to suit local circumstances, have been lost.

Increased food production does not get rid of hunger if poor people do not have money to buy food. Who is actually getting the additional food?

Poorer farmers unable to afford the necessary chemicals, equipment and so on, cannot compete.

Green Revolution policies have increased dependency on imported seeds, fertilisers, pesticides and farm machinery.

Imports of seeds, chemical fertilisers and fuel for machinery all cost valuable foreign currency.

Often agricultural profits are invested in machinery like tractors, which reduces employment.

Small farmers face real hardship from lower prices for their harvests.

Greater use of chemicals has harmed the environment and encouraged pests to become resistant to pesticides.

D) Technology and sustainability ....65

✡ Using what you have learned about the Green Revolution, choose one of the following and explain how it might have come about.

**a** The kinds of changes introduced by the Green Revolution have tended to benefit the more well-off farmers, but harmed poorer ones.

**b** In 1987, it was estimated that 50 percent of the world's hungry people lived in just five countries, four of them in Asia where the Green Revolution has taken place. (Report to the World Commission on Environment and Development, "Food 2000").

# A fragile planet

Take an apple: this represents the world. Cut it into four quarters, vertically. Put three aside — they represent the earth's surface covered by water. Slice the remaining quarter into eight slivers, and discard seven — these represent mountains, deserts etc. where agriculture is not possible. Peel the remaining sliver — that peel represents the earth's surface on which we depend for food, and for survival.

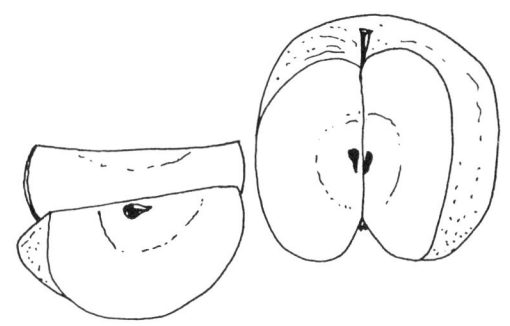

Here is another way to think about the Earth.

✏ Use the words at the bottom to fill in the gaps.

> ❝ We see it like this: it is as if we are all in a _____ travelling through _____. If someone begins to make a _____ in their part of the canoe, and another begins to pour _____ inside the canoe, or another begins to piss in the canoe, it will affect us all. And it is the responsibility of each _____ in the canoe to ensure that it is not destroyed. Our _____ is like one big canoe.... The _____ of the forest is everyone's _____. ❞
>
> Ailton Krenak, Brazilian Union of Indian Nations.

| canoe | concern | destruction | fire |
| person | planet | time | water |

D) Technology and sustainability ....67

# Technology for sustainability

**Sustainable** development is:

> "development that meets the needs of the present without compromising the ability of future generations to meet their own needs."
>
> World Commission on Environment and Development, 1987.

The technology that goes along with that kind of development could be called **appropriate technology.**

Appropriate technology is:

| | |
|---|---|
| **Locally decided** | Designed and controlled by the people who will use it, to suit their needs and wishes |
| **Locally made** | Uses local knowledge, skills and materials as far as possible |
| **Sustainable** | Does not use up the resources it depends on, or solve one problem by creating another |
| **Affordable** | Not too expensive to set up, run or repair; fits within the means of the community |
| **Efficient** | Does what it is set up to do, with a careful, accurate and economical use of resources |
| **Fair** | Does not depend on an unfair share of the earth's resources; could be used even if everyone decided to adopt it. Does not favour one group over another, eg. men over women. |
| **Ecological** | Fits into the earth's natural systems and does not harm the environment |
| **Holistic** | Takes into account the whole picture, and the links between technology and other parts of life |
| **Encouraging self-respect** | Enables people to rely on their own skills and abilities to earn a living, not depend on others |

# Appropriate or inappropriate?

Decide which of the following examples fit the principles of appropriate technology and which do not. Give reasons for your choices.

## Brazil

> ❝ We don't need your electricity. Electricity won't give us food.... We need our forests to hunt and gather in. We don't want your dam. ❞
>
> Kayapo woman to Brazilian official at meeting about Altamira dam.

## Northern Zambia

A traditional system called **chitemene** is used to increase the amount of land available for food production. This involves cutting off the lower branches of trees to allow farming beneath them, rather than uprooting the whole tree which would lead to soil erosion.

## Ladakh, northern India

Household and community level technology based on renewable sources of energy, which Ladakh has in abundance, has been introduced in many villages. For example, solar power is used for space heating units, water heating systems, ovens and crop dryers. All of these are relatively inexpensive, and can be built, installed and maintained by local craftspeople.

## Providenciales Island, Caribbean

Foreign experts have decided that an international airport and holiday village are needed to attract tourists. The benefits these will bring to the island's 1000 people are not clear.

# A final note

Some people in the North have found it easy to blame the South for destroying the environment. This is one Southerner's reply:

> **"** Wouldn't you cut down a tree to cook your next meal if there was no other option? The environment is a luxury; only those who have enough food already have the time to worry about it. You eat the chocolate biscuits — you people who have never seen a cocoa tree. We pick the cocoa beans — we people who have never tasted chocolate biscuits. You worry about the environment. We cut down trees. **"**
>
> Bernard Guri, Co-ordinator of Agricultural Programmes,
> National Catholic Secretariat, Ghana.

⊛ How does Bernard Guri's statement relate to the principles of appropriate technology and sustainable development?

# RECOMMENDED RESOURCES

***City Lights: Fatal Attractions.*** WWF. An investigation of urbanisation issues, with students' resource book and teacher's notes.

***Creating Art, Creating Income: A women's textile workshop in Bangladesh.*** Intermediate Technology. KS 3&4 resource which looks at dyeing and printing processes as well as a small business in Bangladesh. With teacher's notes, 2 slide sets, case study and country information.

***Fala Favela.*** Trocaire, 1991. Photopack which explores issues of power and poverty faced by a shantytown community in Sao Paulo. With 24 A5 colour photos.

***Hanging by a Thread: Trade, debt and cotton in Tanzania.*** Leeds DEC, 1992. An activity pack for 14-19 year olds which explores international trade and debt using cotton production in Tanzania as a case study.

***Kumasi and Beyond.*** Birmingham DEC, 1995. Explores urban development and enterprise in Ghana.

***A Place to Call my Own.*** Crisis and DEP, 1992. An active learning pack on homelessness for 13-16 year olds.

***Shifting Sands: Agriculture, development and environmental change in India's Thar Desert.*** Leeds DEC, 1994. A teaching pack focusing on how the Green Revolution and the Indira Gandhi canal have affected people's lives and the environment. With 24 A4 colour photos.

***Stove Maker, Stove User: Fuel efficient stoves in Sri Lanka.*** Intermediate Technology. KS 3&4 resource which looks at energy issues, the need for more efficient methods of cooking and the making of stoves in resistant materials. With 2 slide sets, teacher's notes, classroom activities, case study and country information.

***Strategies and Guidelines.*** Intermediate Technology. A guide for teachers interested in introducing appropriate technology, global and development issues into the curriculum, with suggestions for classroom activities.

***The Trading Game.*** Christian Aid. A simulation game which shows how the gap between rich and poor countries can be maintained and widened by international trading systems.

***Trading Trainers.*** CAFOD, 1994. A simulation game which explores the links between consumerism and poverty. For ages 14+.

At the time of writing, all of these resources can be supplied mail order by DEP. Contact DEP's Resources and Information Worker for details of prices and availability.

# ABOUT DEP

The Development Education Project (DEP) was set up in 1978 by the United Nations Association. It has a strong local and regional base, working with schools, teachers and advisers throughout the ten Greater Manchester LEAs. It has also gained a reputation for innovative work with a national impact. DEP offers in-service training, provides curriculum development support, produces publications for schools and runs a resource centre.

Through all its work, DEP aims to encourage and develop educational approaches and methods which will

★ enable people to recognise in their own lives the links between North and South, and to acknowledge how much we can learn from one another;

★ increase understanding of the economic, social, cultural, political, environmental and spiritual forces which shape the relationship between North and South and which affect all of us; and

★ enable people to achieve a more just and sustainable world, in their schools and communities as well as more widely, in which power and resources are more fairly shared by all.

For more information about DEP's work, please contact us at

DEP, c/o The Manchester Metropolitan University
801 Wilmslow Road, Didsbury, Manchester M20 2QR.
Telephone: 0161 445 2495
Fax: 0161 445 2360
e-mail: depman@gn.apc.org